Dedicated to the fortitudinous encumbered.

M.D. Tophus

Reasonable Resilience in Workplaces and Healthcare Work.

Hilphma Publications 2022. www.hilphmapublication.com

First Edition.

Germany.

The author has over 25 years of clinical experience in the healthcare field. Is cognisant of both DSM-5-TR (and previous versions) and ICD-11 (and previous versions) disorders and conditions; quality and safety improvement in healthcare; and healthcare education.

Other M.D. Tophus publications available:

"Exercising Quality in Healthcare Service Provision: A Complex Care Workbook for All Healthcare Professionals." Germany: Hilphma Publications: 2022.

"Who is This Colleague?: Dangers of the Healthcare Profession, and beyond. An Interview Guide for Recruitment, Performance Appraisal and Post-Adverse Events."
Germany: Hilphma Publications: 2022.

"Think on your Feet: Those Who Can. For the Consummate Healthcare Professional."
Germany: Hilphma Publications: 2022.

"The Unfortunate Healthcare Treater, The Hapless Healthcare Therapist: Narcissistic and Borderline Personality Disorder clients. The Grit."
Germany: Hilphma Publications: 2022.

"Victims of Crime: Introduction to Forensic Challenges in Healthcare."
Germany: Hilphma Publications: 2022.

"The A to Z of Workplace Bullying: For the Healthcare Professional and Beyond."
Germany: Hilphma Publications: 2022.

"Trauma United, Life Defined. A Healthcare Tool for Professionals Across the Globe."
Germany: Hilphma Publications: 2022.

"Reflective Thinking: the True Healthcare Tool."
Germany: Hilphma Publications: 2022.

"Burnout in Healthcare"
Germany: Hilphma Publications: 2022.

CONTENTS

Resilience is foremost, individual and personal. It involves stamina and adaptability.

Resilience is frequently used and abused to manipulate, justify, and normalise often very unreasonable demands in workplaces, including healthcare environments.

Expectations of invincibility, working till one drops- in the name of the profession or healthcare system- and the accepted standard which entails extreme and almost impossible work conditions (like over extended work hours, poverty of staff and resources), is the epitome of unreasonable resilience.

This concept of resilience differs greatly from what is- and is necessary- to encourage in healthcare workers and affiliated colleagues. True resilience involves, yes- the ability to overcome significant obstacles, withstand great amounts of stress, and yet- have the capacity (and right) to leave work at work.

Healthy, unincentivised, reasonable resilience is thus, to endure with limits whether for the sake of patients, the healthcare facility, personal and, professional, reasons.

It increases the:

-chances of self-awareness

-a sense of purpose

-flexibility.

This publication incorporates reasonable resilience: definitions; in workplaces; in the healthcare system; challenges in individual healthcare fields, law enforcement and emergency services; assessment processes; exemplifications; enhancement methods and activities; and questions. It is written with the intention of assisting increased comprehension of resilience which is reasonable, effective, and do-able within workers, healthcare professionals and affiliated professions, whilst remaining relevant to the readers of all walks of life.

DEFINING REASONABLE RESILIENCE

"Resilience is the process and outcome of successfully adapting to difficult or challenging life experiences, especially through mental, emotional and behavioral flexibility and adjustment to external and internal demands" (1)

It also includes social and physical resilience.

'Reasonable resilience' involves appropriate, non-extreme nor intrusive, demanding expectations of resilience.
It is an adequate response to non-excessive adaptation to challenges and difficulties.
It involves anticipation from others (eg leaders, managers)- of a person- which is rational and even-handed.

Unrealistic anticipation of resilience and, expectancy of invulnerability within individuals, is the antithesis of reasonable resilience.

The 7 pillars of resilience (2), incorporate:

-optimism

-acceptance

-focussing on potential solutions

-responsibility for one's life

-escaping victimhood

-support network

-flexible strategising for future issues

What constitutes medium to high levels of resilience?

<u>**Awareness of your limits:**</u>

-solid personal identity, and truthfulness with self about one's own knowledge, skills and capabilities will naturally ensure safer productivity

-absorbing emotional contagion (from others) can set you on a path toward burnout

-limits involve cognitive, physical, emotional and social factors

-you have the right to feel respected and safe at work

-being everything to everyone weakens resiliency and resolve

-find alternative ways of doing things to reduce stress

-remain true to one's own ethos as best you can

-rely on regulations, policies and guidelines if you are at a loss- remain positive in reminding others

-ensure regular breaks (including mental ones).

Awareness of other's limitations:

-problem-solving for conflicts can be effective but it is not your sole responsibility to solve them

-be cognisant of high conflict personality types

-having a contingency (consequence) plan is helpful when conflicts arise

-expectations and successful reliance on others' productivity can very much depend upon the day

-competing and comparing oneself with others may be helpful for some, but it can place extra burden and pressure on you- compromising resilience resources.

<u>**Ability to recognise stress and manage it before it leads to burnout (3):**</u>

-constant worrying about work

-insomnia, or hypersomnia

-exhaustion

-low energy

-increasing cynicism

-emotionally and physically drained

-resentment

-mood problems

-high levels of anxiety, or depression.

<u>**Determination and fortitude whilst staying true to oneself:**</u>

-Determination, at its core, is:

-For instance, "the most shareable media often capture attention by focussing on negative emotions such as fear, disgust, and moral outrage. Without knowledgeable gatekeepers, opinion can appear as fact, and misinformation can be both monetized and weaponized". (4)

<u>**Some forms of hopefulness to maintain focus on end goals (and short-term ones) which help bring purpose and meaning to your work, and work duties:**</u>

-remind oneself why you entered the profession, the job, the career to start with

-are there elements of your work duties which fulfil (in some way) these objectives

-reflect upon the satisfaction you gain from completing even somewhat menial tasks

-marry up the short-term goals achieved with your plans for the future

-remaining confident in achieving your long-term objectives can assist.

<u>**Accessing support when needed:**</u>

-often there is a culture of shame in not knowing everything

-obviously, knowing all is an impossiblity

-at these times, access to a trusted colleague (or team members) is key to workplace success

-protocols, processes, procedures, style of task provision, and information which is only disseminated by 'word of mouth', are some of the stumbling blocks which workers (in a variety of fields) regularly encounter.

Sufficient self-esteem and self-efficacy levels:

-self esteem is about having confidence in the value of oneself and your workplace (and other) abilities

-having belief in one's own intuition, judgement and decision-making is essential for healthy self-esteem

-self-efficacy is the belief in one's capabilities to be appropriately and effectively productive at work

-it involves confidence in productivity, decision-making and how one presents oneself

-ability to cope with clients' issues, described problems, and fortitude in the interactions which take place, are inclusive

-self-efficacy also involves the capacity to deal with individual idiosyncracies, habits, gestures, and overriding personalities

-likewise, actioned ability and belief in oneself before, during and after, client service provision

-where resiliency stores are low (in addition to minimal levels of self-esteem and self-efficacy), the added pressures of high workload and stressors can push one toward the edge of not coping.

<u>**Contingency planning for meeting challenges effectively:**</u>

-contingency planning is a decisive action plan for any future workplace issues

-they can be in the forms of: prevention of, and response to, problems/incidents and to provide assistance in preventing recurrence

-it is an accepted form of business risk management in numerous fields of work

-assessing risk; cultivating the contingency plan; informing specific workplace groups of the plan; and simulated problem activities, can assist in creating an effective contingency plan

-many workers have an either written, or retained in memory, mini-contingency plan or multiple plans specific to mentally compartmentalised workplace activities.

<u>**Having the physical and mental fuel to frequently cope with issues:**</u>

-enough rest, recuperation time, and sleep

-lifestyle which suits your needs to maintain stability

-debrief as required

-that is, in the manner in which is best for each individual.

<u>Applying resilience training benefits to your personal circumstances (in order for it to be meaningful, long lasting and easily applied to your work, profession and career):</u>

-rote learning of: resiliency factors and actions of resilience, is unhelpful if it is sans insight and inner acceptance.

True resilience training benefits include:

-motivation

-personal awareness of capabilities

-furthering of inner strength

-increased, reasonable productivity at work (and in other aspects of one's life)

-confidence to self-manage tasks, where appropriate.

<u>Resilience takes effort to maintain and can be built on over time:</u>

-reasonable resilience incorporates multiple inner resources which require nurturing and maturing over time.

For instance:

-psychological resilience: withstanding disappointments, and recognising their impermanency

-emotional resilience: being able to temper extreme emotions in the face of adversity

-physical resilience: endurance with- boundaries and acceptable- limits

-cognitive resilience: comprehending, and deciphering, truth from fiction.

It is natural to experience emotions (negative and positive) in response to workplace challenges:

-it is regulation thereof which is key

-this is not to say that one should be expected to be stoic when workplace adversity strikes

-it is about utilising the 7 pillars of resilience (for example) effectively whilst being kind to oneself.

Standing up to, and reporting, damaging issues within the workplace, like bullying (M.D. Tophus 'A to Z of Bullying' covers all forms)(5), toxic colleagues, and clinical errors, is imperative. To avoid doing so, can predispose to weakening of resilience resources across the spectrum.

REASONABLE RESILIENCE in the HEALTHCARE SYSTEM

Resilience in healthcare is "a healthcare system's ability to adjust its functioning prior to, during, or following changes and disturbances, so that it can sustain required performance under both expected and unexpected conditions". (6)

However, it must be stated, that without individual resiliency, there is no system based resilience. The numerous protocols, procedures and guidelines which may be formulated to protect and expand healthcare systems' strengths is the sum of nothing without the unique, and individually special, people who serve to implement healthcare day to day.

Factors which are essential to further resilience in healthcare professionals, include:

-safety in the work environment

-compatability of goals and objectives

-camaraderie, or at least a positive working environment.

Ensuring health and well-being are not tokenistic concepts when it comes to building long-term qualities of resilience. They should not, ideally, be predetermined by another as a pre-requisite (or part of performance appraisals) as a measure of resilience.

Self-paced, self-referred, independent, coping support- based resiliency programmes are the most suitable avenues of learning (where either required, or self-nominated). This is especially where there is a natural reticence to share vulnerabilities within, and between, healthcare teams.

Please see page 32 for reasonable resilience enhancing activities, methods and examples.

REASONABLE RESILIENCE CHALLENGES in INDIVIDUAL HEALTHCARE FIELDS

Psychologists:

-expected to have (with some confident that they do have) immunity to: lapses in, or poor levels of, resilience

-'heal thyself', and maintain the balance regardless, is the overriding thought pattern (toward psychologists) within (and outside) of healthcare environments.

Key challenges to resilience, include:

-constant need for critical thinking skills

-poor supervision

-professional development demands

-emotional effort

-inadequate self-care skills

-toxic: management and organisational milieu.

Nurses:

-caring/caregiving is expected to supplant any feelings of exhaustion and fatigue

-weaponisation of the old concept of vocation then emerges (via managers, leaders, etc), causing potential exploitation and a reduction in resilience.

Primary resilience challenges, involve:

-difficult patients

-significant clinical issues

-physically and verbally abusive clinical interactions

-incidents of abuse unreported, or undocumented

-low autonomy in clinical decision making, and task completion

-medical error blame projected onto nurses

-authoritarian supervisors, managers

-extreme nurse to patient ratios

-inaccessability to support staff

-inaccessability to doctors for sign-off

-double shifts, or minimal breaks between shifts.

Physiologists:

-work is often delegated to, from occupational therapists and physiotherapists

-pecking order/hierarchical challenges where the physiologist is considered to do the leg work post-case planning.

Significant challenges which weaken resiliency levels:

-interdisciplinary rivalry

-organisational management factors

-minimal physical therapy resources, or inaccessability to, for work completion

-unreasonable expectations/goals within patient case planning

-work de-prioritised- other clinical, and therapeutic, tasks take precedence over the physiologist's access to patients

-being kept 'out of the loop', miscommunications or nil communication regarding patient status, clinical planning and tests.

Social Workers:

-some forms of organising, delegating, and work prioritizations, can give a false sense of confidence in one's resilience

Issues challenging resilience may involve:

-patient non-compliance

-time factors relating to delegation of tasks to other allied healthcare workers

-sidelined by primary care professionals during case planning

-unavailable referral resources

-lengthy time between task allocation, referral.

Doctors:

-the perceived holder of life and death in their hands, the invincibility of a doctor is expected at all times

-the constant pressurised decision-making, and expectations of availability, invariably take its toll- weakening resiliency reserves.

Weakening of resilience may incorporate:

-lengthy periods of being on-call

-unrealised accomplishments

-involvement in critical incidents whereby the doctor was in charge

-medico-legal negligence, insurance and malpractice concerns

-professional life impinges upon personal life (personal connections expecting free advice at all times)

-understaffing

-failure to complete, or satisfy, KPIs

-patient resistance.

Moving away from the categories of selfless, self-invested, intrinsically and extrinsically motivated, kindness; proverbial points into heaven; or, traditional vocational versus career angles, the following holds much relevance.

Kindness for the sake of it, without expectation of outward gratitude, reward, or even a reciprocal smile.

Kindness in being able to place oneself in another's position, or shoes.

This reaps its own internal reward.
Nevertheless, when this is mindfully practised- hour after hour, day to day, especially, the necessity of balance with self-care becomes obvious.

Otherwise, compassion fatigue/caregiver burnout can be a risk.

Kindness is however, both a form of resilience and confirmative of resiliency, for the healthcare worker (in particular).

This is a choice. It differs from helpfulness, and although may be included in healthcare professionals' oaths, creeds and pledges, stands very much on its own (by the instigators' choices and actions).

REASONABLE RESILIENCE in PROFESSIONS AFFILIATED with HEALTHCARE (Police, Emergency Services)

Please note, as with the abovementioned professions, the challenges and supportive measures listed below may be interchangeable between professions.

Police/Law Enforcement

Challenges to resilience:

-incessant exposure to highly stressful situations

-experiences of violence, abuse, dangerous incidents (and preparing oneself constantly for the inevitability- hour to hour, shift to shift)

-limited awareness of, capacity to, and opportunities for, expressions of vulnerabilities within policing without stigmatisation, fear of reprisal and, negative impacts upon career.

Supportive measures to maintain and improve levels of resilience include:

-clear understanding of legalities

-human factors based qualities, such as sufficient resources

-effective leadership styles and decision-making

-sense of control regarding work tasks

-supportive partnerships, teams and, workplace culture

-ethical conduct

-positive morality of fellow officers

-good morale within the systemic environment

-availability of critical incident debriefing and stress management programs

-solid personal identity

-clear boundaries observed between work and private life

-sufficient rest and leisure activities

-preparatory training in the form of systematic desensitisation for differing incidents which may arise.

Emergency services/First responders

Resistance challenges include:

-motor vehicle accidents; stabbings; shootings

-disasters (including floods and fires)

-grief, survivor guilt, and sadness, can weaken resilience

-observing human suffering

-risk to life and limb

-working long hours, or multiple shifts.

Supportive measures which may assist in building and maintaining resilience, are:

-disaster, and critical incident, simulation training

-individual coping resources' reinforcement

-regular breaks

-effective routines (such as bedtime; hobbies etc)

-seperation between work, home life, and extra-curricular activities

-system based education regarding stress, coping, and vulnerabilities during and

post-incidents

-highlighting to oneself regularly the enjoyable parts of one's job

-job task variability

-reinforcement of autonomy within one's work duties.

Please see M.D. Tophus publication: 'Trauma United, Life Defined. A Healthcare Tool for Professionals Across the Globe' (7) for detailed coverage of PTSD, CPTSD, SVS and ASD.

RESILIENCE: ASSESSMENT

<u>Connor-Davidson Resilience Scale (CD-RISC):</u>

-measures degree of resilience; "as a predictor of outcome to treatment with medication or psychotherapy, stress management and resilience-building" (8); assesses treatment progress; and, is considered a marker for physiological brain alterations.

-categorises low, intermediate and high resilience levels

-25 items (completion time 5 to 10 minutes)

-brief versions: 10 items; 2 items

-in more than 90 different languages

<u>Brief Resilience Scale (BRS):</u>

-assesses ability to bounce back; or, recover from stress; and, coping.

-6 items

-results: low, normal, high resilience

(9)

<u>**Predictive 6-Factor Resilience Scale (PR6):**</u>

-measures both mental and physical factors in 6 resilience domains (neurobiological model of resilience)

-16 items

-time for completion: 3 minutes

-used by public departments, psychologists, police, emergency services

(10)

<u>**Resilience Scale**</u>

-assessment focus is on strengths (purpose; perseverance; self-reliant qualities; calmness and composure during stressors; aloneness)

-25 items (alternative, the shorter scale: 14 items)

(11)

<u>**Resilience Scale for Adults (RSA):**</u>

-measures protective factors including personal qualities, social and external support in relation to resilience (psycho-social focus in dealing with stressors)

-33 items   (12)

<u>**Scale of Protective Factors (SPF):**</u>

-assesses individual cognitive factors as well as social support and skills, planning behavior, and goal efficacy regarding resilience

-24 items

(13)

<u>**Ego Resiliency Scale- Revised (ER89-R):**</u>

-assesses ego modification of control/ adaptation in response to environmental challenges to resiliency; optimal regulation; openness to life experience

-10 items

(14) and (15)

<u>Brief Resilient Coping Scale (BRCS) (Sinclair 2004):</u>

-assesses coping strategies and ability to adapt to stress (flexibility and problem solving focus)

-4 items

-results: low, medium, high resilient coping levels

(16)

REASONABLE RESILIENCE ENHANCING ACTIVITIES, METHODS, and EXAMPLES

Reasonable resilience involves: Self-awareness; self-regulation; mental agility; strengths of character; connection; and optimism. A building of cognitive and emotional fitness.
(17)

Compassionate interest:

-The terms 'compassion' and 'empathy' are often used interchangeably. This can create confusion, especially in the fast-paced healthcare environment.

-'Compassion' is defined as: the emotions felt when dealing with another's suffering along with being compelled to relieve the suffering.

-The use of which, it is argued, should not be contained to specific healthcare fields. It is not: unacademic, singularly- a calling; only for the hierarchically compromised; solely for end-stage care; or, purely for the 'warm and fuzzy brigade', to express and experience compassion during one's healthcare interactions. It is aligned with one's value system.

-Compassion both contributes to, and is, a result of resilience.

-The challenge remains in describing the practice of compassion. For true compassion cannot be taught- one either possesses the capacity for it, or they do not.

-Examples of compassion within healthcare, include:

   -meaningful comforting of the anxious patient

-problem-solving via the use of critical thinking and emotional intelligence

-treating the patient/client by imagining how you, yourself, would like to be treated

-being fully 'present' in interactions with patients/clients (no matter how brief the encounters).

-As mentioned previously, compassion fatigue is a definite concern when one's resiliency resources are/feel low. This requires immediate attention (for instance, breaks, days off, additional self-care regimens) to allay progression.

-For the differentiation with 'empathy', please see page 34.

<u>Targetted responses are not always shallow. A sense of self-satisfaction prevails:</u>

-Indoctrinated styles of clinical practice, which do not shift with organisational change, are ineffective targetted responses.

-Examples of appropriate targetted responses include, utilisation of:

-patient-focussed models

-up-to-date diagnostics

-new (mainstreamed) treatment techniques

-focus on patients' health, well-being, and quality of life

-cost-effectiveness can be produced efficiently via focus on patient outcomes

-Thereby, eliciting mental and emotional relief related resilience.

<u>Modelling calmness can translate (to the healthcare workers') inner core:</u>

-the ultimate calming technique is if the practitioner, themselves, is calm in thoughts, words, and demeanour

-the key is 'absorption' of patient: emotions, content, and words

-de-catastrophise the patients' concerns, explain the statistics (in lay-mans' terms), where possible, of chance of risk to procedures

-even brief interest in an individual patients' lifestyle, significant relationships, or basic circumstances, can help promote calmness

-provide written documentation, in regards to their condition and future planning, which the patient can follow.

<u>Empathic intention (empathy versus pathos):</u>

-'Empathy' is defined as: having the capacity to comprehend and relate with another person's feelings.

-Examples of empathic intention, can be displayed in action and behaviors, as listed below:

-'I understand'

-alternatively, 'I cannot imagine how it would feel to go through what you are
 experiencing but my thoughts are with you'

-'My patients/clients are my first concern which I cannot express enough'

Pathos, on the other hand, is: aligned with inauthentic pity, such as just for show, or used
in conversational rhetoric.

**Providing insight for patients/clients- into their conditions (regardless of the fact
that it may never be fully shared by patients):**

-however, it is affirmative of (the worker/heathcare professional's) confidence (not in power,
but) in a form of effective caregiving.

**Appreciating and reflecting upon the micro, and macro, of patients (idiosyncracies;
unique likes and dislikes..):**

-cognitively and emotionally personalising and individualising one's patients can help
provide further meaning to your work

-when one is nearing exhaustion, or resiliency stores are low, often the coping style alters
toward visualising a sea of patients in numerical form

-once this occurs, your sense of purpose and quality of work suffers- it creates a
downward spiral toward burnout, inefficiency, and meaninglessness

-the patient senses this, and can become attitudinally averse, non-compliant, and/or it makes for an unpleasantly different practitioner-patient relationship.

-appreciating (or even being silently amused by) your patient's habits, interests and overall demeanour can not only assist in healthily relating to clients/patients and reminding oneself that every one is uniquely human (including yourself).

Relating to, and with, patients/clients- without transference, and counter-transference:

-relating to, and with clients/patients, and the positive impact for healthcare professionals goes without saying

-transference is: inappropriately transferring feelings (from patient/client) toward the healthcare practitioner (this can not only take sexualised forms, but solid identification by the patient of idealising the healthcare worker as perfection, as mother or father, or son/daughter. Many other forms can take place)

-counter-transference is: the reverse (inappropriateness of healthcare provider) of transference

-when a worker's resilience is depleted, recognising transference and counter-transference (and risks toward) are also diminished.

Compartmentalisation of work duties/tasks:

-compartmentalisation involves: maintaining focus, where possible, on one specific thing before moving onto another

-or, seperating issues- even if it means breaking one large issue down into tangible categories

-it is similar to placing tasks into seperate boxes

-the act of compartmentalisation creates a feeling of control, even where tasks may feel never-ending

-the simple act of being able to achieve and proverbially tick things off one by one, gives strength and thus, provides nourishment for resilience.

Unrelenting boundaries, regardless of the above:

-"In general, the concept of boundaries refers to the physical, temporal, emotional, cognitive, and relational limits that seperate one entity from the other" (18)

-set boundaries at the start of the interactions, practitioner-patient relationship, it causes far less stress later

-direct, clear, simplified language to establish boundaries

-be aware that if you are exhausted and fatigued then you may allow boundaries to be crossed more easily due to low energy levels, poor confidence and pessimism

-"Boundary violations (i.e. interruptions) not only hinder the task at hand but direct the individual's attention to a new, interrupting task or demand" (18)

-you do not need to offer explanations (detailed, or otherwise) when you are setting boundaries, especially within the workplace

-be aware of priorities and the time it takes to complete them

-reinforcing boundaries with patients, co-workers (etc) is very important

-saying 'No' to extra work/extraneous duties (within reason) is necessary

-persistent assertiveness is recommended for success in the above regard.

Drawing from inner strength (and the surprise of finding more, within oneself), when a patient/client seems 'broken':

-feeling the core of you (whether it be in a non-religiosity, or spirituality, referenced way, or otherwise)- and drawing from one's inner strength- is vital

-finding even simple, solution-based interventions which one can impart to the patient/client as a supportive measure

-ability to assess patient's brokenness, that is: do they require a suicide perturbation related assessment

-resilience is a never-ending discovery of one's own inner strengths and resources. It can very much 'make or break' you, and this is a journey that can either mould your future resiliency resources and career, or create realisation that you need a 'top-up' or break from your profession, career, or job duties.

<u>**Listening for the unsaid/unspoken:**</u>

-client/patient avoidance of certain topics of discussion in relation to their disease condition, or specifics regarding their health and illness, should create alerts during clinical practice

-often patient avoidance may relate to diagnostic and prognostic indicators

-listening, interpreting, and questioning, will provide the practitioner with a greater sense of: purpose, self-efficacy and contingent planning.

<u>**Patience as a form of peacefulness, a 'breather' (if you like):**</u>

-repeating oneself over and over (even in innovative ways) can have its benefits

-it enables the healthcare worker self-re-assurance

-whilst also providing one with a chance to refocus thoughts on other aspects of the patient's/client's care (in a protracted and paced way) whilst remaining 'with' the patient at all times

-ultimately, it can be a welcome break from the often fast-paced clinical decision-making, interventions and adherence to protocols, which can test resilience on all levels.

<u>**Safe space for clients/patients is a secure space for the actual healthcare worker:**</u>

-modelling of safe, secure, private spaces for clients has its advantages for the healthcare worker as well

-regardless of whether one is required to have multiple workspaces, for clinical practice, the concept of 'owning' (albeit for 15 minutes, or an hour) provides a healthy sense of control over one's environment which will assist in affirming self-esteem, self-confidence and serenity.

<u>**Ability to remain unconquered/ unoffended:**</u>

-often patients/clients can seem very trying. Whether it be that they become excitable, verbally (or other) aggressive, or are just simply argumentative personality types. This can definitely fall outside idiosyncratic attributes

-where one senses that a client/patient 'gets his/her jollies' from winding up the healthcare practitioner, your resilience will become your best friend

-whilst reminding of practitioner-client/patient boundaries, need for mutual respect, and the unhelpfulness of unnecessary acts of control, remaining unoffended (leaving it at the office, if you like) and determination to remain unintimidated, is vital.

The hardness/hardiness which one shares in a collegial environment can be dropped (with relief) when the practitioner is one to one with a patient/client (or other, with patient and carer/family member)

<u>**Remembering that some consultations/sessions are more successful than others:**</u>

-Performance of effective consultations involve "(1) determine the question; (2) establish urgency; (3) look for yourself; (4) be as brief as appropriate; (5) be specific and concise; (6) provide contingency plans; (7) honor thy turf; (8) teach with tact; (9) talk is cheap and effective; and (10) follow-up" (19). *Please note, numerical representations above (aside from (19)) pertain to the actual quote only (are not reference numbers).*

Examples of challenged achievements:

-incomplete clinical evaluation

-differential or problem diagnosing the patient's condition

-critical incident occurred during the consultation

-poverty of information/ information not passed onto the consulting healthcare professional resulting in delayed patient treatment

-case-planning up-ended due to unforeseen circumstances

-low levels of patient health literacy, or language barriers.

<u>**Celebrating autonomy (within consultations/sessions) by mindful relief of choices you can make:**</u>

-Aloneness, or making decisions alone, is frowned upon in multiple countries. It is considered anti-team, anti-solidarity and is looked upon with suspicion.

-Furthermore, the criticism is often gender based- with women considered incapable of making solid decisions, and gaining insight, for their own personal and professional quality gain and inner strength. With men- being considered downright strange, or anti-'one of the boys'.

-Sometimes, though, especially when it comes to personal resilience which feed workplace resilience, it is entirely necessary.

-This is not to say that working as a team, on workplace resiliency, is unnecessary.

-However, if there are robotic, uninsightful team members who are primed by, and given to, authoritarian conceptualisations the difficulties which weaken teams, and healthcare systems, remain at its core- untouched.

<u>**Working together (with patients) in tandem:**</u>

-you have aims, goals and objectives to achieve, and so do the patients and clients

-you have to-do task lists, and likewise the client/patient

Working in tandem with patients involves:

-interprofessional collaboration

-the opposite to 'top-down' medical approach

-shared decision making with patients

-personalisation and individualisation of patient care

-the patient is fully informed in a collaborative way about their point of care

-that is: who their doctor is; that they can speak candidly and be listened to; that their feelings, thoughts and concerns be taken into account; and, to whom they speak with about differing health concerns (as in the cases of co-morbidity).

Necessary, self-instigated but enjoyable creative thought when the client/patient is seemingly 'at their wits' end':

Creative thinking, in these situations, may include:

-encouraging the patient to be independent

-understanding the complexity of the human condition

-developing new and innovative ways of approaching problems

-flexibility of thought and clinical action

-appropriate humour

-confidence in ability to deal with exasperated patient types

-honing in on the co-operative, or hopeful, aspects of the client/patient

-lateral thinking

-if you are inspired then this will be invariably modelled for the patient/client.

<u>Sound healthcare (or other) ethics as a natural part of your work undertakings:</u>

-Healthcare professional ethics was once considered extraneous to healthcare professions as unrealisable or intangible in application of clinical practice.

-In the modern day, it is quite the opposite.

-There are numerous quality healthcare organisations embracing clinical and professional healthcare ethics' principles across the globe.

-Nevertheless, in many older style healthcare facilities and systems, there remains a need for education, cognizance and, recognition of, healthcare ethics' importance in day to day reflection and practice.

-The accepted standards of ethics, are: beneficence, non-maleficence, autonomy and justice

-With such knowledge comes an important additional layer to affirming and building on resiliency stores.

<u>**Accessing of a representative of ethics in your work field:**</u>

-though varying from country to country, "moral case deliberation, ethics rounds, ethics discussion groups and ethics reflection groups" (20) with

-a 'bottom-up' approach appears to be the most beneficial way to facilitate direct access to clinical healthcare workers

-an ethics contact person, specific to resource building, clinical and work environment issues, is most necessary.

<u>**Reflecting on achievements, no matter how small:**</u>

Reflection upon:

-short-term effectiveness, efficiency and success in problem-solving

-academic or training achievements

-infiltrating, and breaking down, problems within difficult clinical cases

-that there are different levels of clinical success

-most patients/clients appreciate your efforts- independent of curative or diagnostic endeavours

-providing some insight into disease status as part of your success

-nevertheless, remembering that "employees with higher perceived overqualification are more likely to feel undervalued and unfairly treated". (21)

<u>Human factors:</u>

-Time factors can de-pressurise situations (accepting that one can only achieve as much as time allows, along with colleagues/any in your profession).

-It draws one away from closing toward 'superman/superwoman' complexes.

<u>Limited/no interruptions during completion of work tasks:</u>

-risks of medical error, inaccurate clinical decision-making, along with high levels of healthcare professional stress, can result from frequent interruptions during completion of one's healthcare work

-where possible, re-affirmation of clinical practice and work task boundaries, reminders to colleagues of commitment to patient safety and promotion of safe, calm, and efficient workplace environments, can be just some of the ways to offset limitation of interruptions intra-task.

<u>Access to immediate recording of details (computer/notes' material):</u>

-this provides many links to above, including re-affirmation of boundaries

-often resources within healthcare facilities are limited. This can include digital accessability to notes, and defective information exchange

-clear, accurate and concise note-taking is essential

-it enables multiple treaters to maintain patient quality and safety standards and reduces the chance of medical errors

-access to handwritten files- is always a vital back-up, incase things go awry with digital recording of patients' notes

-suggestions (of note/file accessability as the norm) in: team meetings, with approachable managers, and re-affirmation of necessity to administrative staff, are several of the avenues one might pursue to ensure consistent document access.

Patient contact person/representative links:

-many hospitals, and clinics, have embraced the concept (and use) of 'walkers' (patient representatives who assist and accompany patients to healthcare related appointments)

-in the majority of countries, non-profit patient groups exist, though healthcare facility accessability varies.

Health literacy (basic) literature accessable to patients:

-avenues for accessing healthcare

-timeliness in seeking healthcare provision, and intervention

-scientifically proven/mainstreamed prevention of worsening disease

-accessability to specific healthcare resources relevant to diagnostic bases of identified illnesses

-clear, defined, simplified explanations and language used to provide information to patients/clients.

Dotting the 'i's and crossing the 't's can be done:

-inspite of all of the above, this is do-able, preferably with support

-routines, own workspace, clear time limits dedicated for papework and administrative duties' completion, can be helpful

-so too, treating the documentation as a summarisation of, and end to, a successful (or, otherwise) days' proceedings.

KPIs can be found if you look hard enough:

-this is naturally, self-explanatory

-it can require some forethought, collegial advice and, comprehensive understanding of diagnostic statistical representations

-though it is acknowledged, if one is feeling pressurised to fulfil specific diagnostic KPIs, it can become a tussle between clinical conscience and implied leadership demands.

All of the aforementioned can contribute to longevity, well-being, affirmation, and building of resilience

Watch for signs of burnout (please see M.D. Tophus publication: 'Burnout in Healthcare' for information)(3).

Explain the key indicators of Reasonable Resilience.

What is meant by the 7 pillars of resilience?
Please name four.

Why is it important to stand up to/report workplace bullying?

Which kind of lifestyle should one have to reinforce reasonable resiliency levels?

What is the meaning of reasonable resilience in the healthcare system?

Which type of resiliency programmes are most suitable?

Describe the challenges encountered by 2 of the five individual healthcare fields mentioned.

What is your perception of the use of 'kindness' in healthcare?

Name 4 supportive measures of reasonable resilience for police officers.

Name 4 supportive measures of reasonable resiliency for emergency services' personnel.

Describe 3 resilience assessment measures.

How can exercising patience help with resilience?

Which human factor helps de-pressurise situations?

How can an ethics representative be effectively utilised (for reasonable resilience in healthcare)?

What is the difference between compassion and empathy?
Explain how each can be relevant to reasonable resilence.

How can demeanour be considered part of a technique?

How can patient idiosyncracies be helpful to a healthcare practitioner?

What is counter-transference?

Provide details of what one can undertake when a client/patient appears broken.

How does autonomy factor into reasonable resilience?

What are the accepted standards of ethics?
Please list the main ones.

Name some of the benefits to limited/no interruptions intra-task?

What is your understanding of 'health literacy' in your immediate work environment?

SCENARIO 1

A nurse has worked for 20 years in healthcare settings.

Their manager suggests that she is not a resilient person.

The workplace definition of resiliency includes: not complaining (or even requesting discussion) when:

-sudden prolonged workplace shifts are scheduled;

-a critical incident occurs and the blame is placed upon the nursing staff involved, that one should not question nor dispute such claims;

-and, there is an assault incident upon a nurse from a patient, or fellow staff member, that this should remain unreported to upper management.

Is the above definition within the realms of reasonable resiliency?
Please explain your reasoning.

What is actually expected of the nurse?

How would you approach the situation?

Which particular reasonable resiliency factors are being exploited, if any?

What are the parameters of kindness in this situation?

<u>SCENARIO 2</u>

A psychologist, also, has worked for 20 years in healthcare environments.

For the past 8 years, they have been given the most harrowing of clinical cases seemingly to benefit more senior psychologists.

This includes family members of homicide victims, rape and sexual assault victims, and domestic violence victims.

What are the resilience advantages for the other psychologists?
Are they part of reasonable resilience?

In the interim of rectifying the unfair caseload situation, in which ways can the psychologist use the experience to build resiliency resources?

What are the risk factors for the particular psychologist?

How does productivity and KPIs come into play?

Which other healthcare professions have 'heal thyself' projected toward them?

Is compartmentalisation useful?

Are there obvious ethics' components (in the above)?
If so, please describe.

Explain the exemplified differences between the expectations of reasonable and unreasonable resilience, in this scenario.

<u>SCENARIO 3</u>

A doctor is in a senior position at a local hospital.

He has worked there for 10 years.

He appears to suffer anxiety when there is non-compliance with his frequently difficult patient care demands.

Which factors represent reasonable resilience, and which do not (please consider the healthcare facility, healthcare system, as well as the individual doctor involved)?

What may occur as a result of the doctor's ongoing anxious reactivity?

What, in your opinion, are reasonable and unreasonable patient care demands?

What do you believe represents non-compliance, and how may it affect individual reasonable resilience?

Where does the exercising of boundaries fit?

- and, the unspoken/unsaid?

Which factors may contribute to contingency planning for the doctor's colleagues?

<h2 align="center"><u>SCENARIO 4</u></h2>

A police officer has worked for 5 years dealing with a community which is known to have a high incidence of domestic violence.

His colleagues display regular frustration with the officer as he de-prioritises almost all domestic violence incidents resulting in fellow officers taking the greater workload.

The police unit has a specialist domestic violence social worker on part-time staff- she has set guidelines for the responding (to alleged domestic violence perpetrations) officers.

The particular police officer scoffs at these guidelines and purposefully goes about ignoring them.

How can the concept of reasonable team resiliency be realised?

Describe the factors of morality and ethics, and its possible affect upon morale, with some reference to the above scenario.

In which ways can the fellow police officers protect their existing resilience resources?

How may interdisciplinary conflict affect reasonable resilience within this unit?

Which human factors' resources can be accessed and utilised to help improve this situation?

ABBREVIATIONS

ASD: Acute Stress Disorder

CPTSD: Complex Post-Traumatic Stress Disorder

PTSD: Post-Traumatic Stress Disorder

SVS: Second Victim Syndrome

REFERENCES

(1) VandenBos, G.R. (2015). APA dictionary of psychology (2nd ed.), Washington D.C.: American Psychological Association.

(2) Rampe, M. (2010), Der R-Faktor, Hamburg & Nordstedt: Books on demand

(3) M.D. Tophus (2022), Burnout in healthcare. Germany: Hilphma Publications.

(4) APS Association for Psychological Science (May/June 2022), Above the din: New APS white paper aims to serve as a "misinformation prevention kit" for policymakers and science communicators, Association for Psychological Science, Vol 35(3): 37-39.

(5) M.D. Tophus (2022), The A to Z of workplace bullying: For the healthcare professional and beyond. Germany: Hilphma Publications.

(6) Hollnagel, E., Braithwaite, J. and Wears, R. (Editors) (2013), Resilient health care. Boca Raton: CRC Press, p.xxv

(7) M.D. Tophus (2022), Trauma united, life defined. A healthcare tool for professionals across the globe. Germany: Hilphma Publications.

(8) CDRISC: The Connor-Davidson Resilience Scale (2022), www.connordavidson-resiliencescale.com

(9) Smith, B.W., Dalen, J., Wiggins, K., Tooley, E., Christopher, P. and Bernard, J. (2008), The brief resilience scale: assessing the ability to bounce back. International Journal of Behavioral Medicine, 15(3): 194-200.

(10) Rossouw, P.J. and Rossouw, J.G. (2016), The predictive 6-factor resilience scale: Neurobiological fundamentals and organizational application, International Journal of Neuropsychotherapy, 4(1): 31-45.

(11) Wagnild, G.M. and Young, H.M. (1993), Development and psychometric. Journal of Nursing Measurement, 1(2): 165-178.

(12) Friborg, O., Hjemdal, O., Rosenvinge, J. and Martinussen,M (2003), A new rating scale for adult resilience: What are the central protective resources behind healthy adjustment? International Journal of Methods in Psychiatric Research, 12(2): 65-76.

(13) Ponce-Garcia, E., Madewell, A.N. and Kennison, S.M. ((2015), The development of the scale of protective factors: Resilience in a violent trauma sample. Violence and victims, 30(5): 735-755.

(14) Block, J., and Kremen, A.M. ((1996), IQ and ego-resiliency: conceptual and empirical connections and seperateness. Journal of personality and social psychology, 70(2): 349

(15) Alessandri, G., Letzring, T., Vecchione, M. and Caprara, G. (2012) The Ego Resiliency Scale Revised. European Journal of Psychological Assessment 28(2): 139-146.

(16) Sinclair, V.G. and Wallston, K.A. (2004), The development and psychometric evaluation of the Brief Resilient Coping Scale Assessment, 11(1): 94-101.

(17) Positive Psychology Center (2022), PENN resilience program: Resilience skill set. University of Pennsylvania. www.ppc.sas.upenn.edu

(18) Kerman, K., Korunka, C. and Tement, S. Special issue: Work and home boundary violations during the COVID-19 pandemic: The role of segmentation preferences and unfinished tasks. Applied Psychology: An international review, Vol.71(3): 784-806.

(19) Cohn, S.L. The role of the medical consultant. Med Clin N. Am, 87 (2003): 1-6.

(20) Rasaol, D., Skovdahl, K., Gifford, M. and Kihlgren, A. Clinical ethics support for healthcare personnel: An integrative literature review. HEC Forum (2017), 29: 313-346.

(21) Wu, C-H., Weisman, H., Sung, L-K., Erdogan, B. and Bauer, T.N. Special issue: Perceived overqualification, felt organizational obligation, and extra-role behavior during the COVID-19 crisis: The moderating role of self-sacrificial leadership. Applied Psychology: An international review, Vol.71(3): 983-1013.

INDEX

identification 36

idiosyncracies 14; 35; 51

idiosyncratic 40

ignoring 56

illness 39

illnesses 48

imagine 35

imagining 33

immediate 33; 46; 52

immunity 20

impact 36

impacts 25

impart 38

impermanency 16

implement 18

implied 49

important 38; 44

impossibility 13

improve 25; 56

inaccessability 21; 22

inaccurate 46

inappropriately 36

inappropriateness 36

inauthentic 35

incapable 42

incidence 56

incident 53

incidents 15; 25; 26; 56

independent 19; 43; 45

indicators 39

individual 38; 50; 55

individual resiliency 18

individualisation 43